American Slangs Handbook

Speak Like a Native, From Classic to Modern Terms

Dane Wells

Table Of Content

5

Introduction

What is Slang?

Language is alive. It evolves, breathes, and grows with the people who use it. Among its most vibrant and dynamic forms is slang—those colorful, unconventional words and phrases that refuse to be confined to the formal walls of grammar textbooks. Slang is more than just language; it's a snapshot of culture, a living, breathing expression of how people communicate in a specific time, place, and social setting.

Slang can be playful, irreverent, creative, and deeply meaningful. It takes the formal and makes it informal. It takes the serious and makes it fun. When you hear someone say, "That party was lit!" or "I'm lowkey tired," you're witnessing language at its most flexible—adapting to the needs of the moment, reflecting shared understanding, and creating instant connections.

At its core, slang is informal language—words, idioms, and expressions that are often born in specific groups but spread like wildfire when they resonate. It can arise from youth culture, music, technology, movies, or even social media trends. Slang doesn't always play by the rules, but that's its beauty. It's a rebel in the linguistic world—shifting, morphing, and constantly reinventing itself.

Consider a word like "cool". It has been a staple of American slang for decades, yet its meaning can shift depending on tone and context. "That's cool" might mean approval, admiration, or simply that something meets expectations. Another example is "ghosted", a modern term born in the digital age, describing someone disappearing from a relationship without a trace—like a ghost. These words convey specific meanings with striking clarity, often more so than formal expressions ever could.

Slang fills the gaps in language that formal words sometimes miss. It communicates emotions, reactions, and ideas with immediacy. It makes language fun, relatable, and real. When you understand slang, you're not just learning words—you're learning how people live, laugh, and connect.

The Importance of Understanding American Slang

Why does slang matter, you might ask? The answer lies in its power to connect. Language is the bridge between people, and slang, as a dynamic form of language, adds layers of meaning, familiarity, and identity to our everyday interactions.

For anyone looking to truly understand American culture—whether as a native, a visitor, or someone learning English—understanding slang is essential. Imagine walking into a room where friends are casually throwing around words like "bet," "lit," "salty," or "no cap". If you're not familiar with these terms, the conversation might feel like a foreign language. But once you decode slang, it opens up a whole new world of connection and belonging.

Slang often serves as a social marker. It distinguishes insiders from outsiders. In many ways, it's a secret handshake, a way of identifying who "gets it" and who doesn't. Knowing slang makes you sound more natural, more relatable, and more confident in casual interactions.

Think about it: If you're visiting a new city or country, knowing just a few slang phrases can transform your experience. You'll go from feeling like an outsider to feeling like part of the crowd. For instance, understanding that "y'all" is a friendly, inclusive way to say "you all" in the South, or that "hella" is a West Coast way to emphasize something, immediately brings you closer to the people around you.

For non-native English speakers, learning American slang is especially powerful. While formal English might help you in business or academics, slang will help you connect with people on a personal level. It's the language of friendships, jokes, and everyday life. Without it, even a fluent speaker might feel out of place in casual settings.

Moreover, slang helps you keep up with cultural trends. Much of today's slang emerges from internet culture, social media, and pop culture. Words like "stan" (an obsessive fan) or "FOMO" (fear of missing out) didn't exist in common usage a few years ago but are now part of everyday vocabulary. Staying updated with slang ensures you're not left behind as language evolves.

In short, understanding American slang isn't just about learning words; it's about understanding people—their humor, their culture, their way of life. It's the difference between merely speaking English and truly living it.

How Slang Reflects Culture and Evolves Over Time

Slang is a mirror held up to society. It reflects our values, our struggles, our humor, and our creativity. Every slang term carries with it a piece of the culture from which it was born.

Historically, slang has often emerged from marginalized or subcultural groups before being adopted into mainstream language. For instance, much of modern slang has roots in African American Vernacular English (AAVE), hip-hop culture, and the LGBTQ+ community. Words like "throwing shade" (to subtly insult someone) or "slay" (to do something exceptionally well) highlight how subcultures shape language and influence broader society.

Slang also evolves alongside societal changes. Consider how technology and social media have shaped modern slang. Words like "DM" (direct message), "ghosted," and "troll" didn't exist in their current context 20 years ago. They're products of the digital age, reflecting how we live, communicate, and interact today.

Similarly, generational differences give rise to unique slang. Baby Boomers popularized words like "groovy" and "far out." Gen X gave us "rad" and "dude." Millennials introduced phrases like "adulting" (managing adult responsibilities), while Gen Z brought terms like "bet" (a casual way to agree) and "bussin'" (something really good). Each generation puts its stamp on language, creating expressions that capture their experiences and perspectives.

Slang also reflects the playful nature of human communication. People enjoy creating and sharing new words that are clever, witty, or ironic. Sometimes these words stick around, while others fade into obscurity. For example, terms like "jive" from the 1930s or "groovy" from the 1960s may feel dated now, but they were once at the heart of American culture.

The evolution of slang reminds us that language is never static. It changes as we change. It adapts to new technologies, cultural shifts, and generational attitudes. This constant reinvention is what keeps language alive, fresh, and relevant.

When you understand slang, you're not just keeping up with language—you're keeping up with life itself.

How to Use This Handbook

This handbook is your ultimate guide to American slang. Whether you're a student, a traveler, a non-native speaker, or simply someone who wants to sound more natural in casual conversations, this book has something for you.

Here's how you can get the most out of it:

1. Learn Slang by Category: This book is organized into sections that group slang terms by type and context. You'll find chapters on Classic Slang that has stood the test of time, Modern Slang that you'll hear in today's conversations, Regional Slang that highlights how language varies across the United States, and Internet Slang that dominates digital communication.

2. Understand the Meaning and Usage: Each slang term comes with a clear definition, an example sentence, and a brief explanation of its origin or cultural significance. You'll learn not just what the words mean but how and when to use them.

3. Test Yourself: At the end of the book, you'll find fun quizzes and exercises to help reinforce what you've learned. These activities will challenge you to use slang in practical scenarios, making it easier to incorporate into your daily conversations.

4. Stay Curious: Slang is constantly changing. Use this book as a foundation, but keep your ears open for new terms and phrases. Pay attention to how people speak in movies, music, social media, and everyday life.

By the time you finish this book, you'll have a solid grasp of American slang—from timeless classics to the trendiest phrases of today. You'll not only understand the words but also the culture and history behind them. Most importantly, you'll feel confident using slang naturally, whether you're chatting with friends, traveling, or navigating social media.

So, get ready to dive into the exciting, ever-changing world of American slang. By the end of this journey, you'll speak the language of the streets, the screen, and everything in between.

Welcome to the American Slangs Handbook. Let's get started!

Chapter 1

The Origins of American Slang

The History and Evolution of Slang in the United States

Slang is as old as language itself, yet its role and significance have grown more pronounced with the development of modern societies. In the United States, slang has been a crucial part of the country's linguistic landscape, reflecting its cultural diversity, historical events, and social transformations. To truly understand American slang, one must trace its roots back to the origins of the United States as a melting pot of languages, cultures, and influences.

The Early Years
The earliest American slang can be traced to the colonial period of the 17th and 18th centuries, when settlers from various European countries brought their languages, dialects, and expressions to the New World. The colonies were a mixture of English, Dutch, German, French, and Spanish speakers, along with enslaved Africans and Indigenous communities. This linguistic diversity laid the foundation for a unique blend of language.

At this time, slang often emerged as a means of informal communication among the lower classes—laborers, sailors, and traders—who lived in bustling ports and towns. It was functional, rough, and grounded in daily life. For example, sailors developed their own terms, such as "scuttlebutt" (meaning gossip) and "aloft" (referring to going upward), many of which entered common usage over time.

19th Century: The Rise of American Identity
As the United States declared independence and expanded westward, slang evolved alongside the nation's growing identity. The 19th century was a period of innovation, frontier exploration, and urbanization, all of which brought new linguistic influences. With people constantly moving, trading, and settling in new territories, slang became a tool of communication across diverse populations.

The American frontier, in particular, became a breeding ground for colorful expressions. Words like "buckaroo" (a cowboy, derived from the Spanish vaquero) and phrases like "bite the dust" (to fail or be defeated) reflected the hardships and adventures of life on the frontier. Meanwhile, urban centers like New York City developed their own slang, shaped by immigrants and industrial workers.

It was during this era that American slang began to differentiate itself from British English. The United States prided itself on its cultural independence, and language was no exception. Words like "okay"—one of the most famous American slang terms—originated in the early 19th century as a playful abbreviation of "oll korrect" (an intentionally humorous misspelling of "all correct"). This period also saw the popularization of words like "boss" (meaning excellent) and "dude" (originally a term for a city slicker, now a universal term for "guy").

20th Century: Slang Goes Mainstream
The 20th century was a golden age for American slang, driven by technological advancements, cultural shifts, and the rise of mass media. The early 1900s saw the emergence of jazz culture, with African American communities pioneering slang terms that became staples of the language. Words like "cool," "jive," and "hip" spread from jazz clubs to mainstream society, carrying with them a sense of style, rebellion, and individuality.

World War I and World War II further accelerated the evolution of slang. Soldiers developed their own terms to describe life on the battlefield, many of which entered common parlance. For example, "trench coat" originated from the gear worn in World War I trenches, and phrases like "snafu" (an acronym for Situation Normal, All Fouled Up) reflected the chaos of war.

By the mid-20th century, the explosion of youth culture brought about a new wave of slang. The 1950s gave us words like "cool cat" and "rock 'n' roll", thanks to the influence of music and teenage rebellion. The 1960s and 1970s saw the rise of countercultural slang, with phrases like "far out," "groovy," and "bummer" reflecting the laid-back and anti-establishment sentiments of the era.

The latter half of the 20th century introduced slang tied to technology and entertainment. Words like "geek," "nerd," and "surf" (as in surf the web) emerged alongside the digital revolution, while movies, TV shows, and hip-hop music brought slang into mainstream consciousness.

By the end of the century, slang was no longer confined to small subcultures—it was everywhere, embedded in music, movies, television, and advertising.

Influence of Immigration, Music, and Movies

The United States is a nation built by immigrants, and nowhere is this diversity more evident than in the evolution of American slang. Immigration, combined with cultural forces like music and movies, has played a pivotal role in shaping and spreading slang throughout the country and beyond.

The Role of Immigration

Immigration has brought waves of new languages, ideas, and expressions into American society. Each immigrant group contributed its own words and phrases to the linguistic melting pot, which were often adapted into American English slang.

For example, German immigrants gave us words like "pretzel" and "delicatessen", while Yiddish-speaking Jewish immigrants contributed expressions like "schmooze" (to chat informally) and "glitch" (a small malfunction). Similarly, Italian immigrants popularized terms like "moolah" (money), and Spanish-speaking communities introduced words such as "barrio" (neighborhood) and "macho" (a strong or tough man).

The African American experience has also been a driving force in the development of American slang. From the era of slavery to the rise of jazz, blues, and hip-hop, African American Vernacular English (AAVE) has enriched American English with expressions that often reflect resilience, creativity, and cultural pride. Terms like "cool," "bling," "shade," and "woke" are rooted in AAVE but have been embraced across society.

The Influence of Music
Music has long been a vehicle for popularizing slang. From jazz in the 1920s to hip-hop in the 21st century, American music has introduced countless slang terms into mainstream culture.

Jazz and Blues: In the early 20th century, jazz musicians developed a unique slang that reflected their world of creativity, improvisation, and style. Words like "cool", "cat" (a musician), and "gig" (a performance) originated in jazz circles but quickly spread to broader audiences.

Rock 'n' Roll: The rebellious spirit of rock music in the 1950s and 1960s gave rise to phrases like "rock on" and "hippie", as youth culture rejected traditional norms and embraced a new vocabulary of freedom and self-expression.

Hip-Hop and Rap: Since the 1980s, hip-hop music has been the most significant force in shaping modern American slang. Words like "dope," "homie," "swag," and "flex" entered the mainstream through rap lyrics, television, and movies. Hip-hop has a global influence, making American slang a cultural export to other countries.

Movies and Television
Hollywood has been another powerful engine for spreading American slang. From classic films to modern streaming series, American movies and television shows introduce slang to audiences worldwide.

For example, movies from the 1950s popularized words like "daddy-o" and "square" (someone uncool), while teen comedies from the 1980s, like Clueless, brought phrases such as "as if" and "totally rad" into everyday usage. Television shows like Friends and The Fresh Prince of Bel-Air further embedded slang terms into the public consciousness, with phrases like "How you doin'?" and "chill out" becoming part of the global lexicon.

Today, streaming platforms, social media influencers, and viral content continue to spread slang at an unprecedented rate. Phrases born in online communities, like "spill the tea" (share gossip) and "no cap" (no lie), quickly make their way into movies, music, and casual conversations.

How Slang Spreads: Regional and Global Impact

Slang is a powerful tool for communication, and its spread can be traced through regional differences, cultural influences, and global connectivity.

Regional Slang in the United States
The United States is a vast country, and its regions often develop their own unique slang. These regional differences reflect local cultures, histories, and identities.

The South: Southern states are known for expressions like "y'all" (you all), "fixin' to" (about to), and "bless your heart" (a polite yet sometimes sarcastic phrase).

Southern slang reflects the region's warmth, hospitality, and unique pace of life.

The Northeast: Cities like Boston and New York have their own slang. Terms like "wicked" (very) and "jawn" (a general term for a thing, used in Philadelphia) are examples of Northeastern speech patterns.

The Midwest: Midwesterners are known for friendly, understated phrases like "ope" (an exclamation, often used when bumping into someone) and "pop" (soda).

The West Coast: West Coast slang includes terms like "hella" (a lot or very) and "gnarly" (cool or extreme), which reflect the region's laid-back, surf-and-skate culture.

The Global Spread of American Slang
Thanks to globalization, American slang has become an international phenomenon. Hollywood movies, American music, and social media platforms have exported slang to every corner of the world. Words like "cool," "selfie," "awesome," and "OK" are now universally understood, transcending language barriers.

In many countries, young people adopt American slang to connect with global pop culture and express modern ideas. Social media platforms like TikTok and Instagram accelerate this process, spreading phrases like "lit," "bussin'," and "on fleek" to global audiences in a matter of days.

However, while American slang spreads globally, it often adapts to local contexts, blending with regional languages and cultures to create something entirely new. This process—called linguistic borrowing—shows how slang evolves and thrives across borders.

Chapter 2

Classic American Slangs

Timeless Expressions from the 20th Century

Classic American slang represents a golden era of informal language—words and phrases that stood the test of time, resonating across decades. These expressions often stemmed from specific cultural movements, such as the Jazz Age, the Beat Generation, the counterculture of the 1960s, and the rise of youth-oriented pop culture in the 1980s and 1990s. They reflected not just linguistic creativity but also a window into how Americans lived, thought, and rebelled in the 20th century.

What makes these slang terms "classic" is their longevity. While many slang expressions fade quickly as they lose relevance, others retain their charm, continuing to evoke nostalgia and cultural resonance. Phrases like "cool", "groovy", "rad", and "the cat's pajamas" not only dominated their respective eras but still hold a place in American lexicon today, often invoked with a sense of fun or irony. They have a timeless quality because they're tied to movements, ideas, and cultural shifts that defined American life for decades.

These terms give us insight into the social pulse of each era. For example, the post-World War II optimism of the 1950s gave rise to lighthearted, upbeat slang, while the countercultural movements of the 1960s and 1970s ushered in a more free-spirited vocabulary. By the time the 1980s and 1990s arrived, slang mirrored the fast-paced, vibrant pop culture of the modern age. Each decade added new expressions to the American lexicon, many of which became etched into the cultural fabric.

Understanding these timeless expressions means understanding the spirit of their time. They offer a glimpse into the attitudes, humor, and priorities of generations past, while also reminding us how language can be playful, poetic, and deeply reflective of culture.

Examples, Meanings, and Usage in Sentences

To appreciate classic American slang, it's helpful to see these words in context. Below are some of the most iconic terms of the 20th century, their meanings, and examples of how they were used in conversation.

Cool

Meaning: Calm, impressive, stylish, or admirable. Originating in the jazz scene of the 1940s, the term "cool" was adopted by musicians to describe something stylish, impressive, or "in the know." Over time, its meaning broadened and became universally positive.

Example: "Did you see James Dean in Rebel Without a Cause? He's so cool."

Usage in Conversation: "That jacket looks cool, man. Where'd you get it?"

"Cool" has remained one of the most enduring slang terms of all time. Its simplicity and versatility have allowed it to transcend generations, with new meanings layered onto it over time. Whether describing a person's demeanor or approving of something fashionable, "cool" remains timeless.

Groovy

Meaning: Stylish, excellent, or exciting. Popularized during the 1960s counterculture, "groovy" came from jazz slang, where it initially referred to a musician being "in the groove" during a performance. It became synonymous with anything positive or exciting during the hippie movement.

Example: "That new Beatles record is groovy!"

Usage in Conversation: "This party is totally groovy. The music is amazing."

"Groovy" encapsulates the free-spirited vibe of the 1960s. While its usage declined after the 1970s, it still conjures images of tie-dye shirts, peace signs, and a time when people embraced life's pleasures with optimism and creativity.

Far Out

Meaning: Unbelievable, impressive, or extraordinary. Like "groovy," "far out" is strongly associated with the 1960s counterculture, where it described something fantastic, unusual, or ahead of its time.

Example: "Did you hear Jimi Hendrix play at Woodstock? That was far out!"

Usage in Conversation: "You went skydiving? That's far out, man!"

"Far out" reflects the experimental and unconventional attitudes of the 1960s. The phrase is often used today in nostalgic contexts or as a nod to its origin, evoking a sense of wonder or admiration.

The Cat's Pajamas

Meaning: Something outstanding, impressive, or the best. Originating in the 1920s, "the cat's pajamas" was one of many quirky phrases popularized during the Jazz Age. It belongs to a family of expressions like "the bee's knees" and "the cat's whiskers", all of which praised something exceptional.

Example: "That new dance hall is the cat's pajamas!"

Usage in Conversation: "You've got a new car? That's the cat's pajamas!"

This phrase reflects the playfulness and whimsy of 1920s slang, when the youth embraced jazz music, dance, and fun after the restrictions of World War I. Though rarely used today, it still brings a nostalgic smile and a nod to the linguistic creativity of the past.

Rad

Meaning: Excellent, exciting, or cool. Short for "radical," the term became widely popular during the 1980s skateboarding and surfing subcultures. It was used to describe something impressive or thrilling.

Example: "Your trick on the skateboard was totally rad!"

Usage in Conversation: "This new video game is rad. You have to try it."

"Rad" perfectly captures the upbeat, youth-driven culture of the 1980s and 1990s. Its association with extreme sports, music, and entertainment made it a staple of teen vocabulary. Even today, "rad" occasionally resurfaces as a retro expression.

Cultural Context: The 1950s to 1990s

The development and use of classic American slang cannot be separated from the cultural and historical events that shaped each decade. From the optimistic post-war years of the 1950s to the rebellious spirit of the 1960s and the consumer-driven culture of the 1980s, slang evolved as a reflection of society's changing attitudes, values, and lifestyles.

The 1950s: Optimism and Cool
The 1950s marked a period of economic prosperity and cultural transformation in America. With World War II in the rearview mirror, the country experienced a baby boom, suburbanization, and a sense of optimism. This decade saw the rise of rock 'n' roll, personified by icons like Elvis Presley, and the emergence of teenage culture as a distinct force.

Slang terms like "cool", "daddy-o", and "hip" reflected this newfound youthful confidence. Young people sought to define themselves in contrast to their parents, embracing music, fashion, and attitudes that were fresh and exciting. James Dean, the quintessential "cool" rebel of the 1950s, epitomized the era's slang with his effortless style and demeanor.

The 1960s and 1970s: Counterculture and Grooviness
The 1960s and 1970s were defined by cultural upheaval. The civil rights movement, anti-Vietnam War protests, and the sexual revolution created a spirit of rebellion and social change. The counterculture movement, led by hippies, promoted peace, love, and self-expression, giving rise to slang terms like "groovy," "far out," "trippy," and "dig it".

Music played a central role in shaping the slang of this era. Bands like The Beatles, The Rolling Stones, and Jimi Hendrix popularized new ways of speaking that resonated with the youth. The language of the counterculture rejected formality, celebrating instead a free-spirited and experimental approach to life.

The 1980s and 1990s: Pop Culture and Radness
By the 1980s and 1990s, American society had shifted toward consumerism, technology, and pop culture. MTV brought music videos into every home, movies like Back to the Future and The Breakfast Club shaped teen culture, and extreme sports became a phenomenon.

Slang terms like "rad," "awesome," "gnarly," and "totally" emerged from surf and skateboarding subcultures but quickly entered mainstream vocabulary. These expressions reflected the upbeat, high-energy spirit of the time, where everything was bigger, brighter, and louder.

The 1990s, driven by grunge music, sitcoms like Friends, and the rise of hip-hop, introduced slang that reflected a mix of irony and coolness. Phrases like "whatever" (dismissive indifference), "phat" (excellent), and "all that" (something impressive) dominated casual conversations.

Key Words: Cool, Groovy, Far Out, Cat's Pajamas, Rad

These five classic slang terms—cool, groovy, far out, the cat's pajamas, and rad—are emblematic of the 20th century's cultural and linguistic evolution. They reflect how American slang adapted to different movements, attitudes, and generational shifts.

"Cool" remains universal, representing calmness and admiration across generations.

"Groovy" captures the creative, free-spirited nature of the 1960s.

"Far out" reflects the wonder and experimental vibe of the counterculture era.

"The cat's pajamas" highlights the playful energy of the Jazz Age.

"Rad" speaks to the fast-paced, vibrant culture of the 1980s and 1990s.

Each term has a unique story, tied to the music, movies, and movements of its time. Together, they serve as linguistic landmarks, reminders of how slang can encapsulate a moment in history and remain beloved long after its peak

Chapter 3

Modern American Slangs

Popular Terms in the 21st Century

The 21st century has ushered in a new era of slang, characterized by its rapid evolution, increased accessibility, and deep ties to technology. Unlike the slower spread of slang in previous centuries, modern terms can go viral almost overnight, thanks to the internet, social media platforms, and globalized communication. Slang in this era is not limited to a specific region or subculture but instead travels seamlessly across borders and generations.

Modern American slang reflects the fast-paced, hyper-connected nature of contemporary life. It is often playful, witty, and versatile, constantly adapting to cultural trends, memes, and technology. Today's slang resonates with younger generations, especially Gen Z and millennials, who create, use, and redefine language daily through their interactions online and offline. Words like "lit," "lowkey," "sus," and "ghosted" have become universal expressions, transcending their origins to enter mainstream conversations.

What makes 21st-century slang unique is its ephemeral nature. A phrase might rise to popularity within days, peak for a few months, and then fade into obscurity, replaced by the next trending term. However, some words manage to achieve staying power, cementing their place in modern lexicon because they perfectly capture a cultural phenomenon, behavior, or feeling.

The slang of this era is deeply reflective of contemporary society's focus on self-expression, humor, and relatability. Whether used in text messages, viral TikTok videos, or casual conversations, these terms embody the creative and dynamic way people communicate in the digital age.

Internet and Social Media Influences

The rise of the internet and social media has completely transformed the way slang develops, spreads, and solidifies itself in popular culture. In earlier decades, slang emerged slowly through music, movies, and regional interactions. In the 21st century, platforms like Twitter, Instagram, TikTok, YouTube, and Snapchat serve as incubators for slang, rapidly spreading new terms to millions of people worldwide.

Social media fosters the creation of slang because it encourages brevity, creativity, and relatability. People look for quick and catchy ways to communicate complex feelings, reactions, or ideas in limited character spaces. Hashtags, captions, memes, and viral trends often give birth to new slang terms that reflect a moment in time. For example, words like "flex" and "extra" became mainstream partly because they were used widely in humorous memes and relatable TikTok videos.

Another significant influence of the internet is its ability to democratize slang. In previous decades, regional dialects or niche subcultures dictated the development of slang, but now anyone with a smartphone can create or popularize a new word. A tweet, a viral video, or a celebrity post can introduce a term that gains widespread traction within hours.

Memes, in particular, are a driving force behind modern slang. Words like "salty" or "bet" often become embedded in internet culture before transitioning to everyday speech. Memes make slang more accessible, relatable, and entertaining, encouraging people to adopt new phrases to connect with others.

Social media also creates a sense of community through shared slang. Online users embrace certain words because they create an "insider language" that allows them to bond with others who understand the references. This digital camaraderie fuels the rise of terms like "lowkey" or "ghosted", which reflect specific emotions or situations that are universally relatable.

Examples, Definitions, and Real-Life Usage

Understanding modern American slang involves exploring not just the words themselves but also their meanings, origins, and how they are used in everyday life. Below are some of the most popular and widely used slang terms of the 21st century, complete with definitions and examples of usage.

Lit

Meaning: Amazing, exciting, or fun. Something that is "lit" is highly enjoyable or impressive.

Origin: "Lit" originally referred to someone being intoxicated or "lit up," but its modern usage expanded to describe exciting events or moments.

Example: "That concert last night was lit!"

Usage in Conversation: "Your birthday party looks lit in those photos. I wish I'd been there!"

"Lit" is one of the most versatile modern slang terms. It can describe anything from a party to a performance, a situation, or even someone's personality. Its positive connotation makes it a go-to word to express enthusiasm.

Lowkey

Meaning: Subtle, quiet, or slightly. "Lowkey" is used to downplay something or suggest that it is not overly dramatic but still relevant.

Origin: The term gained popularity on social media, where users needed a word to express feelings that weren't extreme.

Example: "I lowkey love staying in on weekends."

Usage in Conversation: "I'm lowkey nervous about that presentation tomorrow."

"Lowkey" perfectly captures the modern trend of understated self-expression. It allows people to share thoughts or feelings in a way that feels casual, relatable, and unpretentious.

Sus

Meaning: Suspicious or shady. "Sus" describes someone or something that seems untrustworthy, odd, or sketchy.

Origin: The term gained traction through gaming culture, particularly the popular game Among Us, where players accused others of being "sus" (suspicious) if they appeared guilty.

Example: "He didn't show up for work today, and his story sounds sus."

Usage in Conversation: "You're acting sus. What are you hiding?"

"Sus" is a great example of how gaming culture influences modern slang. It has since transcended its origins and is now widely used to describe anything questionable or uncertain.

Ghosted

Meaning: To suddenly stop all communication with someone without explanation.

Origin: "Ghosted" comes from the idea of someone disappearing like a ghost, leaving no trace behind. It gained popularity in the context of modern dating.

Example: "I thought we were getting along, but then she ghosted me."

Usage in Conversation: "I haven't heard from him in weeks. He totally ghosted me."

"Ghosted" reflects the modern dating landscape, where communication often happens digitally. It describes the frustrating experience of being ignored or abandoned without closure.

Flex

Meaning: To show off or brag, often about possessions, achievements, or wealth.

Origin: "Flex" comes from hip-hop culture, where artists use it to describe flaunting their success or style.

Example: "Posting that luxury car on Instagram was a huge flex."

Usage in Conversation: "I'm not trying to flex, but I just got promoted at work."

"Flex" highlights the role of social media in shaping modern slang. The term often appears in contexts where people showcase their lifestyles or accomplishments online.

Extra

Meaning: Over-the-top, dramatic, or excessive.

Origin: "Extra" emerged as a way to describe people or behaviors that are exaggerated or unnecessarily elaborate.

Example: "She's so extra—did you see that gown she wore to a casual dinner?"

Usage in Conversation: "I know I'm being extra, but I want everything to be perfect for the party."

"Extra" resonates with modern sensibilities, where people value self-expression and humor. It's often used playfully to describe situations or personalities.

Salty

Meaning: Bitter, annoyed, or upset, often over something trivial.

Origin: "Salty" dates back to older slang describing someone as sharp or irritable, but it gained new popularity through internet memes.

Example: "He got salty when he lost the game."

Usage in Conversation: "Don't get salty just because you didn't win the argument."

"Salty" is a humorous way to describe pettiness or irritation. It often appears in lighthearted contexts, adding a playful tone to disagreements.

Bet

Meaning: Affirmation, agreement, or a challenge. "Bet" can mean "okay," "I agree," or "watch me prove it."

Origin: The term stems from African American Vernacular English (AAVE) and gained widespread usage through social media.

Example: "You think I can't do it? Bet."

Usage in Conversation: "You'll be there on time? Bet—I'll see you then."

"Bet" reflects the modern trend of brevity and assertiveness in language. Its multiple meanings make it a versatile and powerful expression in casual conversations.

Key Words: Lit, Lowkey, Sus, Ghosted, Flex, Extra, Salty, Bet

The slang terms lit, lowkey, sus, ghosted, flex, extra, salty, and bet perfectly encapsulate the nature of modern American slang. They are short, relatable, and versatile, allowing people to express emotions, reactions, and ideas with minimal effort. These words have become integral to everyday conversations, both online and offline, because they capture specific feelings or situations that resonate with contemporary life.

Lit celebrates excitement and positivity.

Lowkey embraces subtlety and casual honesty.

Sus calls out suspicion or uncertainty.

Ghosted highlights the challenges of modern communication and dating.

Flex reflects the culture of showcasing achievements and lifestyles.

Extra humorously critiques over-the-top behaviors.

Salty playfully points out irritation or bitterness.

Bet affirms confidence, agreement, or a challenge.

These words continue to evolve as new trends and cultural shifts emerge. Modern American slang will likely keep changing as quickly as the world itself, driven by technology, creativity, and a desire to connect. By understanding these terms, we gain a deeper appreciation for the way language reflects the energy and ingenuity of contemporary society.

Chapter 4

Regional Slangs Across the United States

Southern Slang: Y'all, Fixin' to, Bless Your Heart

The Southern United States is well-known for its distinct cultural identity, warm hospitality, and unique linguistic flair. Southern slang reflects the charm, politeness, and laid-back lifestyle of the region, which encompasses states like Texas, Georgia, Alabama, Louisiana, and the Carolinas.

One of the most iconic Southern slang terms is "y'all," a contraction of "you all." It is commonly used as a plural second-person pronoun and serves as a friendly, inclusive way to address a group of people.

Example: "Are y'all coming to the barbecue this weekend?"

The appeal of "y'all" lies in its simplicity and warmth. Unlike "you guys" or "you all," it feels inherently welcoming and rolls off the tongue with ease. This word has spread beyond the South and is now embraced nationwide, often as a more gender-neutral option for group address.

Another hallmark of Southern speech is the phrase "fixin' to," which means "getting ready to" or "preparing to do something." It reflects the Southern emphasis on pacing life with intention and care.

Example: "I'm fixin' to head to the store. Do you need anything?"

This expression may seem unusual to outsiders, but it highlights the regional preference for colorful, descriptive language. "Fixin' to" transforms a mundane activity into something worth announcing, emphasizing a sense of thoughtfulness and preparation.

The phrase "bless your heart" epitomizes Southern nuance. It is one of the most versatile—and often misunderstood—expressions in Southern slang. Depending on the context, tone, and delivery, it can convey genuine sympathy, subtle sarcasm, or polite disdain.

Example: "Oh, you tried to fix the car yourself? Bless your heart."

In this case, the phrase is a polite way of acknowledging someone's effort while implying that the outcome wasn't ideal. Southern speakers masterfully use such expressions to maintain politeness while conveying layered meanings.

The South's linguistic charm lies in its rhythm, hospitality, and wit. Words like "y'all," "fixin' to," and "bless your heart" carry cultural weight and reflect the region's values of friendliness, community, and respect. Southern slang is a celebration of tradition, storytelling, and the art of speaking with intention.

Northeastern Slang: Wicked, Mad, Jawn

The Northeastern United States, which includes states like Massachusetts, New York, Pennsylvania, and New Jersey, boasts a linguistic style that is sharp, energetic, and often influenced by urban life. Northeastern slang reflects the region's fast pace, rich history, and cultural diversity.

One of the most famous slang words from the Northeast—particularly in Boston and parts of New England—is "wicked." In this context, "wicked" functions as an intensifier, meaning "very" or "extremely."

Example: "It's wicked cold outside today!"

The origins of "wicked" as slang trace back to its use in Boston, where it became a defining feature of the regional dialect. Unlike other intensifiers like "really" or "super," "wicked" adds a unique edge that reflects the character of the Northeast.

Another popular term is "mad," which is often used in New York and surrounding areas as an intensifier, similar to "wicked." It conveys emphasis in a straightforward, no-nonsense way.

Example: "That pizza place is mad good. You've got to try it."

The use of "mad" highlights the Northeast's preference for direct, impactful language. It reflects the region's emphasis on efficiency and clarity while maintaining a casual tone.

A standout slang term unique to Philadelphia is "jawn." "Jawn" is a versatile, catch-all noun that can refer to virtually anything—a person, place, object, or situation.

Example: "Pass me that jawn over there."

Usage: "Did you see that new jawn they built downtown?"

The beauty of "jawn" lies in its flexibility. It reflects the creativity and adaptability of the region's language, serving as a linguistic shortcut that resonates deeply with Philadelphians.

Northeastern slang is punchy, direct, and expressive, reflecting the urban energy and cultural richness of the region. Words like "wicked," "mad," and "jawn" capture the wit, ingenuity, and resourcefulness that define the Northeast's approach to communication.

West Coast Slang: Hella, Bro, Gnarly

The West Coast, particularly California, is synonymous with a laid-back, sun-soaked culture that influences its slang. West Coast language reflects the region's easygoing vibe, its connection to surf and skate culture, and its openness to innovation and creativity.

One of the most iconic West Coast slang terms is "hella." Popularized in Northern California, particularly in the Bay Area, "hella" means "very" or "a lot."

Example: "That concert was hella fun!"

The word "hella" perfectly captures the casual, enthusiastic tone of West Coast communication. It conveys a sense of excitement without feeling overly formal or exaggerated.

Another popular West Coast term is "bro." While "bro" is used nationwide, it holds particular significance on the West Coast, where it reflects the region's relaxed, friendly culture.

Example: "What's up, bro? You coming to the game later?"

On the West Coast, "bro" transcends its literal meaning to serve as a term of endearment, camaraderie, and connection. It underscores the laid-back attitude of coastal life.

The word "gnarly" is rooted in California surf culture, where it originally described challenging waves. Over time, its meaning expanded to describe anything extreme, impressive, or shocking—both positively and negatively.

Example: "That skate trick was gnarly, dude!"

Usage: "The traffic on the 405 today was gnarly."

"Gnarly" reflects the influence of outdoor and adventure culture on West Coast slang. It carries a sense of awe, excitement, and intensity, making it a versatile term for describing experiences.

West Coast slang is laid-back, friendly, and vibrant, much like the region itself. Words like "hella," "bro," and "gnarly" embody the relaxed energy, creativity, and optimism that define the West Coast lifestyle.

Midwestern Slang: Ope, You Betcha, Pop

The Midwest, often referred to as "America's Heartland," encompasses states like Minnesota, Wisconsin, Michigan, Ohio, and Illinois. Midwestern slang reflects the region's practicality, politeness, and strong sense of community.

One of the most endearing and recognizable Midwestern expressions is "ope." Used as a polite, almost reflexive interjection, "ope" often surfaces when someone bumps into another person, drops something, or makes a minor mistake.

Example: "Ope, sorry about that—I didn't see you there!"

"Ope" captures the Midwest's reputation for politeness and humility. It's a linguistic quirk that feels uniquely Midwestern and often brings a smile to those familiar with it.

Another common Midwestern phrase is "you betcha," which conveys agreement, enthusiasm, or reassurance.

Example: "Are you coming to the potluck tonight?"
"You betcha!"

This phrase reflects the region's friendly and agreeable nature. It serves as a charming, upbeat alternative to simply saying "yes" or "sure."

The term "pop" is another hallmark of Midwestern slang. While other parts of the United States refer to carbonated beverages as "soda" or "Coke," Midwesterners use the term "pop" almost exclusively.

Example: "Do you want a pop with your burger?"

The use of "pop" highlights the regional loyalty to traditional terms and reflects the straightforward, no-frills attitude of Midwesterners.

Midwestern slang is unassuming, practical, and filled with warmth. Expressions like "ope," "you betcha," and "pop" reflect the politeness, friendliness, and community-oriented values that are hallmarks of Midwestern life.

How Geography Shapes Language

The regional variations in American slang highlight the profound impact of geography, history, and culture on language. Each region's unique experiences, lifestyles, and values shape the way people speak, creating linguistic identities that are deeply rooted in their environments.

In the South, the slower pace of life and emphasis on hospitality give rise to warm, expressive language. Terms like "y'all" and "bless your heart" reflect a culture that values community, politeness, and storytelling.

The Northeast's urban energy and cultural diversity fuel direct, impactful slang like "wicked," "mad," and "jawn." These words mirror the region's fast pace, creativity, and adaptability.

On the West Coast, the influence of surf culture, technology, and laid-back living shapes slang like "hella," "bro," and "gnarly." The language reflects a lifestyle that embraces adventure, openness, and innovation.

In the Midwest, the region's practicality, politeness, and close-knit communities inspire terms like "ope," "you betcha," and "pop." These expressions embody the region's charm, humility, and straightforward communication.

Geography also determines how slang spreads and evolves. Coastal regions, with their exposure to immigration, trade, and global influences, often introduce new slang that gradually moves inland. Meanwhile, isolated areas may preserve older expressions and regional quirks for longer periods.

Technology and modern transportation have blurred some regional boundaries, allowing slang to travel more quickly than ever before. Yet, regional dialects remain strong because they carry cultural pride, history, and identity. People often hold onto their unique phrases as a way of honoring their roots and distinguishing themselves from others.

Language is a living, breathing reflection of the people who speak it. Regional slang across the United States showcases the nation's diversity, creativity, and sense of belonging. It serves as a reminder that where we come from—our geography, culture, and experiences—shapes not only how we speak but also who we are.

Chapter 5

Internet, Social Media, and Gen Z Slangs

How Online Culture Creates New Expressions

The rise of the internet and social media platforms has transformed how we communicate, leading to the rapid creation and adoption of new slang. Unlike traditional slang, which often developed regionally or within specific subcultures, internet slang emerges from a global digital space where millions of people interact in real time. Online culture acts as an incubator for new expressions, providing endless opportunities for creativity and experimentation with language.

Social media platforms like Twitter, TikTok, Instagram, and Reddit play a pivotal role in shaping these linguistic trends. Memes, viral videos, and online challenges often introduce slang that spreads rapidly across different demographics. Unlike traditional word-of-mouth communication, where slang might take years to gain popularity, the internet enables words and phrases to become mainstream within days.

A defining characteristic of online culture is its visual and interactive nature. Emojis, GIFs, and memes often serve as visual representations of slang, reinforcing their meaning and making them accessible to a global audience. For instance, the expression "no cap" (meaning "no lie" or "for real") is often accompanied by a baseball cap emoji crossed out, adding a visual element that strengthens its context.

Moreover, online culture thrives on brevity. Platforms like Twitter, with its character limit, encourage concise communication, while TikTok emphasizes quick, engaging content. This environment fosters the creation of short, punchy slang terms that are easy to type, remember, and share.

Another factor driving the creation of internet slang is its adaptability. Online culture allows users to remix and redefine existing phrases, giving them new meanings in different contexts. For example, the word "stan" originated as a reference to Eminem's 2000 song about an obsessive fan but has since evolved to mean a devoted supporter of someone or something. This fluidity keeps internet slang dynamic and ever-evolving, reflecting the fast-paced nature of online interactions.

In essence, online culture has democratized language creation. Anyone with a social media account can contribute to the development of new slang, whether through a viral tweet, a catchy TikTok sound, or a humorous Reddit post. This open-source approach to language ensures that internet slang remains diverse, innovative, and reflective of the digital age.

Abbreviations and Acronyms: LOL, FOMO, DM, SMH

Abbreviations and acronyms are a hallmark of internet and social media communication. They provide a quick and efficient way to express emotions, reactions, and ideas, catering to the fast-paced nature of online interactions. These shorthand expressions have become so embedded in digital culture that many are now recognized and used in spoken language as well.

One of the earliest and most enduring examples is "LOL," which stands for "laugh out loud." Originating in the early days of online chatrooms, LOL quickly became a go-to way to indicate humor or amusement. While its original meaning remains intact, LOL has also evolved into a conversational filler, often used to soften statements or convey a lighthearted tone.

Example: "I'll be late, LOL. Traffic is crazy."

Another widely used acronym is "FOMO," which stands for "fear of missing out." FOMO captures the anxiety many people feel when they perceive others are experiencing something enjoyable or important without them. Social media amplifies this feeling by constantly showcasing curated highlights of other people's lives.

Example: "I couldn't make it to the party last night, and now I have serious FOMO after seeing everyone's posts."

"DM" (direct message) has become a standard term for private conversations on social media platforms. Its simplicity and utility make it indispensable in online communication, whether for personal or professional purposes.

Example: "If you're interested, send me a DM, and we'll discuss the details."

"SMH," short for "shaking my head," is another acronym that conveys disapproval, frustration, or disbelief. It is often used to react to situations or comments that are perceived as foolish or annoying.

Example: "They canceled the concert at the last minute. SMH."

These abbreviations highlight the efficiency and immediacy of internet communication. They allow users to convey complex emotions and ideas in just a few characters, making them ideal for text-based interactions. Furthermore, their widespread adoption demonstrates how internet slang bridges the gap between digital and real-world communication.

Viral Trends: Cap/No Cap, IYKYK, Stan, Bussin'

The internet thrives on viral trends, and many slang terms gain popularity through their association with memes, challenges, or cultural phenomena. These expressions often originate from specific communities or platforms but quickly become mainstream due to their relatability and versatility.

One such term is "cap" and its counterpart "no cap." Derived from African American Vernacular English (AAVE), "cap" means "lie" or "falsehood," while "no cap" signifies honesty or truthfulness. This phrase gained prominence on social media and in hip-hop culture, where it is frequently used to assert authenticity.

Example: "That movie was the best of the year, no cap."

Usage: "You said you'd help me move, but now you're ghosting me? That's cap."

"IYKYK," short for "if you know, you know," is another popular internet slang term. It hints at an inside joke or shared experience, creating a sense of exclusivity among those who understand the reference.

Example: "That concert last night… IYKYK."

The term "stan" exemplifies how online communities shape language. Originally referring to an obsessive fan, "stan" has evolved to describe anyone who passionately supports or admires someone or something. It often carries a playful or self-aware tone, acknowledging the intensity of modern fandoms.

Example: "I stan this new album—it's a masterpiece!"

Another viral term is "bussin'," which means exceptionally good or delicious, especially when referring to food. This word gained traction on TikTok, where users frequently use it in reaction videos or food reviews.

Example: "This pizza is bussin'—best I've ever had!"

These viral slang terms illustrate the power of the internet to amplify language trends. Platforms like TikTok, Twitter, and Instagram act as megaphones, enabling niche expressions to reach global audiences.

Once a term goes viral, it often transcends its original context and becomes a staple of internet communication.

How Slang Travels Globally Through Social Media

Social media has revolutionized how slang spreads, breaking down geographical and cultural barriers to create a truly global exchange of language. In the past, slang often remained confined to specific regions or subcultures, spreading slowly through face-to-face interactions. Today, platforms like Twitter, Instagram, and TikTok allow slang to travel across the world almost instantaneously.

One key factor in this global spread is the accessibility of social media. With billions of users worldwide, platforms provide a space where people from diverse backgrounds can interact and share linguistic trends. A single viral video or tweet can introduce a new slang term to audiences in different countries, sparking a chain reaction of adoption and adaptation.

The use of hashtags, challenges, and trends further accelerates this process. For example, a hashtag like #NoCap can create a centralized hub for users to explore and engage with content related to the term. As users from different cultures participate, they often add their own interpretations and nuances, enriching the slang's meaning and usage.

Another driving force behind the global spread of slang is the influence of pop culture. Movies, music, and television shows often serve as vehicles for introducing slang to international audiences. When a song featuring terms like "bussin'" or "stan" goes viral, listeners around the world begin incorporating these words into their own vocabularies.

However, the global adoption of slang also raises questions about cultural appropriation and linguistic authenticity. Many internet slang terms, particularly those rooted in AAVE, gain widespread popularity without proper acknowledgment of their origins. While this demonstrates the universal appeal of slang, it also highlights the need for cultural sensitivity and respect in the digital age.

Social media's impact on language extends beyond English. Non-English-speaking communities frequently create their own slang, which can gain international recognition through translation or context. For example, the Korean term "aegyo" (meaning cute or charming) has found a global audience thanks to the popularity of K-pop and Korean dramas.

Ultimately, social media has transformed slang into a shared global phenomenon. It allows people from different cultures to connect, collaborate, and innovate, creating a dynamic linguistic landscape that continues to evolve with each viral trend and hashtag. The internet has made the world smaller, and in doing so, it has made our language richer, more diverse, and more interconnected than ever before.

Chapter 6

Slang in Pop Culture

Slang from Movies, TV Shows, and Music

Pop culture has long been a powerful engine for creating and popularizing slang. Movies, TV shows, and music serve as cultural touchstones, introducing new expressions that resonate with audiences and often become part of everyday language. These mediums not only reflect the evolving dynamics of language but also amplify specific phrases, allowing them to transcend their original contexts and become embedded in popular consciousness.

Movies are particularly influential in shaping slang, as they often encapsulate the spirit of their time. Iconic lines from classic films have introduced expressions that endure for decades. For instance, the phrase "Here's looking at you, kid" from Casablanca became an enduring romantic expression, while "May the Force be with you" from Star Wars entered the lexicon as a way to wish someone luck. These expressions were not just catchphrases but symbols of the cultural moments they represented, immortalized by the massive reach of cinema.

Similarly, TV shows have acted as incubators for slang. Comedy series, in particular, excel at introducing quirky, humorous expressions that quickly gain traction. Shows like Friends popularized phrases like "How you doin'?" through Joey Tribbiani's flirtatious delivery, while The Simpsons gave us "D'oh!" as Homer Simpson's signature exclamation of frustration. These terms often gain further cultural momentum as fans repeat them in conversations, memes, and social media posts.

Music, too, plays a crucial role in spreading slang. Artists often draw from their personal experiences, regional dialects, or subcultural identities to coin new terms that resonate with listeners. Hip-hop, in particular, has been a major influence, with its rich tradition of wordplay, double entendre, and linguistic creativity. Songs by artists like Tupac, Notorious B.I.G., Jay-Z, and Beyoncé have introduced phrases that not only reflect urban culture but also become mainstream expressions.

Through these mediums, pop culture serves as both a mirror and a megaphone for slang. It reflects the creativity of language while amplifying it on a global scale, ensuring that certain expressions achieve a level of universality that transcends borders and generations.

Memorable Catchphrases and Their Impact

Catchphrases from movies and TV shows have an unparalleled ability to shape language, often gaining a life of their own outside the context of their original works. These memorable phrases capture the essence of a character, scene, or emotion, making them instantly relatable and repeatable. As audiences adopt and adapt these lines, they become cultural shorthand for specific situations, emotions, or attitudes.

One of the most iconic examples is Clint Eastwood's "Go ahead, make my day" from the movie Dirty Harry. Delivered with a mix of defiance and confidence, the line quickly became a cultural symbol of empowerment and challenge. Even people who haven't seen the movie recognize the phrase, demonstrating its broad cultural penetration.

Similarly, the phrase "Bazinga!" from The Big Bang Theory became synonymous with playful trickery or a lighthearted joke. Sheldon Cooper's distinctive delivery of the line made it an instant hit, and it soon became a popular way for fans to punctuate their own pranks or jokes.

Other catchphrases, like "I'll be back" from The Terminator, not only defined the characters who delivered them but also became symbols of determination and resilience. The widespread repetition of these lines highlights their versatility and universal appeal.

These catchphrases often transcend their original contexts through memes, merchandise, and social media trends. They become tools for self-expression, allowing people to connect with others by referencing a shared cultural moment. Their impact is a testament to the power of storytelling and the ability of well-crafted dialogue to leave an indelible mark on language and culture.

Examples: "Make My Day" (Dirty Harry), "Bazinga!" (The Big Bang Theory)

Clint Eastwood's "Go ahead, make my day" from the 1983 film Sudden Impact (part of the Dirty Harry series) is one of the most iconic lines in cinematic history. Its enduring popularity lies in its simplicity and emotional resonance. The phrase is a declaration of confidence and control, delivered in a moment of tension that perfectly encapsulates the character's no-nonsense attitude. Over time, it has been repurposed in countless contexts, from politics to advertising, showcasing its adaptability and universal appeal.

In contrast, "Bazinga!" from The Big Bang Theory represents a more playful approach to language. Used by Sheldon Cooper to signal that he's made a joke or pulled a prank, the phrase captures the character's quirky sense of humor. Fans of the show embraced the term, incorporating it into their own vernacular as a way to express surprise or delight. Its widespread adoption demonstrates how humor and relatability can turn a simple word into a cultural phenomenon.

Both of these examples highlight the diverse ways in which pop culture contributes to the evolution of slang. While "Go ahead, make my day" represents the dramatic, larger-than-life power of cinema, "Bazinga!" showcases the playful, intimate connection that TV shows can create with their audiences. Together, they illustrate the wide-ranging influence of pop culture on language.

Music and Hip-Hop Influences on Slang

Music, particularly hip-hop, has been one of the most influential forces in shaping modern slang. Since its emergence in the 1970s, hip-hop culture has introduced countless expressions that reflect the creativity, resilience, and identity of the communities from which it originated. Artists use slang as a way to tell their stories, celebrate their roots, and connect with their audiences.

Hip-hop's impact on slang is evident in phrases like "bling" (referring to flashy jewelry), "dope" (meaning excellent or impressive), and "woke" (indicating awareness of social and political issues). These terms, originally rooted in African American Vernacular English (AAVE), gained mainstream recognition through the music of artists like Jay-Z, OutKast, and Kendrick Lamar.

Example: "That new track is so dope—it's on repeat all day!"

Beyond individual words, hip-hop has popularized entire linguistic styles, including the use of metaphor, rhyme, and rhythm to create new meanings. Phrases like "drop the mic" (indicating a triumphant conclusion) and "spit bars" (referring to rapping skillfully) have become part of everyday language, demonstrating the genre's influence on how people express themselves.

In addition to its linguistic contributions, hip-hop has also played a role in democratizing slang. Through its global reach, the genre has introduced regional expressions to international audiences, fostering cross-cultural exchange and understanding. For instance, terms like "squad" (a close group of friends) and "throw shade" (to subtly insult someone) have been embraced by listeners around the world, thanks to their inclusion in popular songs.

Other genres of music, including rock, pop, and country, have also contributed to the evolution of slang. The 1960s saw the rise of terms like "groovy" and "far out" in rock and psychedelic music, while contemporary pop artists like Taylor Swift and Billie Eilish have introduced phrases that resonate with younger audiences.

The relationship between music and slang is a dynamic one, with each influencing the other in a continuous cycle of creativity and innovation. As artists push the boundaries of language, they inspire their listeners to do the same, ensuring that slang remains a vibrant and integral part of cultural expression.

Chapter 7

Slang for Everyday Situations

At Work: Circle Back, Low-Hanging Fruit, Crush It

The workplace has its own unique slang, often blending professional jargon with informal expressions to create language that is concise, relatable, and sometimes even humorous. Over the years, office environments have embraced a variety of phrases that reflect the dynamics of teamwork, productivity, and strategy. These terms often serve as shorthand for complex ideas or processes, making communication quicker and more efficient.

One common phrase in the workplace is "circle back." This term means to revisit a topic or discussion at a later time, often when more information or context is available. It's a polite way of delaying a decision or conversation without dismissing it entirely.

Example: "Let's circle back to this after we gather more data from the client."

"Circle back" has become a staple in office meetings and emails, symbolizing the iterative nature of business discussions. Its widespread use demonstrates how workplace slang can create a shared understanding among colleagues.

Another frequently used term is "low-hanging fruit," which refers to tasks or goals that are easy to achieve and offer quick results. It's often used in brainstorming sessions or strategy meetings to prioritize simple, high-impact actions.

Example: "Let's focus on the low-hanging fruit first to build momentum for the project."

This phrase reflects the practicality of modern work culture, emphasizing efficiency and results. It's a metaphorical reminder to tackle the easiest wins before moving on to more challenging objectives.

Finally, the phrase "crush it" has gained popularity as an expression of encouragement or praise. It means to excel at a task or perform exceptionally well, often in the context of a presentation, deadline, or sales goal.

Example: "Great job on the pitch today—you absolutely crushed it!"

"Crush it" embodies the high-energy, motivational language often found in workplaces, particularly in industries like tech, sales, and startups. It's a way of celebrating achievements and inspiring others to give their best effort.

Workplace slang like these examples not only simplifies communication but also fosters a sense of camaraderie among team members. By using shared expressions, colleagues can build rapport and create a more relaxed, collaborative environment.

Social Settings: I'm Down, Chill, Hang Tight

In social settings, slang plays a crucial role in setting the tone and building connections. It reflects a sense of informality and mutual understanding, helping people navigate interactions with ease. Whether making plans, offering reassurance, or expressing agreement, these casual expressions add flavor to everyday conversations.

One popular term in social contexts is "I'm down." This phrase means that someone is willing or eager to participate in an activity or agree with a suggestion. It conveys enthusiasm and a laid-back attitude, making it a favorite among friends and peers.

Example: "You want to grab pizza later? I'm down!"

"I'm down" exemplifies the flexibility and openness that often define casual social interactions. It's a simple yet effective way to signal agreement or excitement without overcomplicating the conversation.

Another versatile term is "chill," which can function as a noun, verb, or adjective. As a noun or verb, it refers to relaxing or spending time leisurely. As an adjective, it describes something or someone as cool, easygoing, or nonchalant.

Example (noun/verb): "Let's just chill at my place tonight."

Example (adjective): "I like her vibe—she's super chill."

The word "chill" captures the essence of relaxation and ease, making it a go-to expression for describing casual plans or laid-back personalities. Its adaptability ensures its continued relevance in everyday language.

"Hang tight" is another slang term often used to reassure someone or ask for patience. It implies waiting calmly for something to happen, often in situations where a solution or update is on the way.

Example: "We're working on your order right now—just hang tight for a few more minutes."

This phrase is a gentle way of acknowledging someone's anticipation while encouraging them to remain calm. Its informal tone makes it suitable for both friendly and slightly more formal exchanges.

Social slang like these expressions helps create a sense of familiarity and ease in conversations. They allow speakers to convey emotions, intentions, and attitudes in a way that feels natural and relatable.

Travel and Shopping: This is a Steal, Road Trip, Ripped Off

Travel and shopping experiences are rich with slang that captures the excitement, challenges, and occasional frustrations of these activities. From planning a journey to scoring a great deal, these expressions enhance the storytelling and emotional resonance of such moments.

The phrase "this is a steal" is often used to describe an item that is priced far below its perceived value. It conveys a sense of triumph at finding a bargain and is commonly used during shopping trips or when sharing purchase stories.

Example: "I got these designer shoes for $50—this is a steal!"

"This is a steal" reflects the joy of getting more for less and highlights the thrill of bargain hunting. It's a phrase that resonates with shoppers who pride themselves on their ability to spot great deals.

"Road trip" is another term that has become synonymous with adventure and spontaneity. It refers to a journey taken by car, often for leisure or exploration. The phrase evokes images of freedom, camaraderie, and the open road, making it a beloved expression for travelers.

Example: "We're planning a road trip to the Grand Canyon next weekend—can't wait!"

"Road trip" captures the spirit of travel in a way that feels personal and relatable. It's not just about the destination but also the experiences and memories created along the way.

On the flip side, the term "ripped off" describes the feeling of being overcharged or deceived in a transaction. It's often used to express frustration or disappointment after realizing that something wasn't worth the price paid.

Example: "I paid $20 for a tiny cup of coffee—I feel so ripped off!"

"Ripped off" serves as a cautionary expression, reflecting the occasional pitfalls of shopping or traveling. It's a reminder to be vigilant and discerning, especially in unfamiliar settings.

These travel and shopping slang terms add color to the stories we tell about our experiences. They capture the highs and lows of these activities, making them more engaging and relatable for others.

Practical Tips for Using Slang Naturally

While slang can enhance conversations and help build connections, using it effectively requires an understanding of context, tone, and audience. Misusing slang or overusing it can come across as awkward or inauthentic, so it's important to strike the right balance.

One key tip is to match your slang usage to the setting and the people you're speaking with. In casual environments with friends or peers, slang is usually welcome and can even strengthen bonds. However, in more formal settings, such as professional meetings or unfamiliar social circles, it's best to use slang sparingly and with caution.

Another important consideration is authenticity. Slang often reflects a speaker's personality, background, or cultural influences, so it's essential to use expressions that feel natural to you. For instance, if you're unfamiliar with a term or its nuances, it's better to avoid using it until you've observed how others use it in context.

Additionally, it's helpful to stay updated on current slang trends, especially if you're interacting with younger generations or participating in online communities. Language evolves rapidly, and keeping up with the latest expressions can make your conversations more relevant and engaging.

Finally, be mindful of cultural and regional differences in slang. Expressions that are common in one area or group may not be understood—or may even be misinterpreted—in another. When in doubt, ask for clarification or choose more universal language to avoid misunderstandings.

Using slang naturally is about blending it seamlessly into your communication style. When done well, it can add warmth, humor, and relatability to your interactions, helping you connect with others on a deeper level. Whether at work, in social settings, or during travel and shopping adventures, slang is a valuable tool for expressing yourself and building relationships.

Chapter 8

The Do's and Don'ts of Using Slang

When to Use Slang and When Not To

Slang is a versatile and dynamic part of language, but its use requires careful consideration of the context. While slang can add personality and relatability to conversations, it is not universally appropriate. Knowing when to use slang—and when to avoid it—can make a significant difference in how you are perceived by others.

Slang works best in informal settings where the tone is relaxed and the participants share a common cultural or social understanding. For example, among friends, family, or peers, using slang can help you build rapport, express emotions, or convey humor. Phrases like "I'm down" or "chill" can make interactions feel more authentic and relatable. However, even in these informal contexts, it's important to ensure that the slang you use is familiar to your audience to avoid confusion or alienation.

In contrast, slang is often out of place in formal settings. Professional environments, academic discussions, or interactions with individuals unfamiliar with the slang may require more standard language. For instance, using phrases like "circle back" or "low-hanging fruit" in a business meeting is generally acceptable because they are workplace slang. However, injecting casual expressions such as "lit" or "bet" into a corporate presentation might undermine your credibility.

Cultural sensitivity is another critical factor to consider. Slang that is acceptable in one region or social group may not translate well to others, and certain terms can carry unintended connotations. For example, words that are harmless in one country might be offensive in another, so it's essential to be mindful of your audience's background.

Ultimately, the decision to use slang should depend on your goals for the conversation. If your aim is to connect on a personal level, slang can be a powerful tool. However, if clarity, professionalism, or universality is your priority, sticking to standard language is often the better choice.

Slang in Casual vs. Professional Settings

The distinction between casual and professional settings is one of the most important factors in determining the appropriateness of slang. Each context has its own expectations for tone, vocabulary, and communication style, and understanding these differences can help you navigate social and professional interactions effectively.

In casual settings, slang thrives as a form of self-expression and social bonding. Whether you're at a party, chatting with friends, or engaging in online conversations, slang adds flavor and personality to your speech. It helps you convey emotions, humor, and relatability in ways that formal language cannot. For example, phrases like "that's fire" or "it's a vibe" can instantly communicate enthusiasm or approval in a way that feels natural and engaging.

However, even in casual settings, it's important to be mindful of your audience. Overly niche or regional slang may confuse people who are not familiar with the terms, and using outdated expressions can make you appear out of touch. Striking the right balance involves choosing slang that feels authentic to you while ensuring it resonates with the people you're speaking to.

Professional settings, on the other hand, demand a more measured approach to slang. While certain workplace expressions like "circle back" or "think outside the box" are widely accepted, overly casual or trendy slang can come across as unprofessional. For example, saying "this idea is lit" during a team meeting might make you seem less credible, even if your enthusiasm is genuine.

That said, some workplaces—particularly in creative industries or startups—may encourage a more relaxed communication style, where slang can be used to foster a sense of camaraderie and innovation. In these environments, it's still crucial to gauge the tone and preferences of your colleagues before adopting slang in your professional vocabulary.

The key to using slang effectively in any setting is adaptability. By assessing the expectations of your environment and tailoring your language accordingly, you can ensure that your use of slang enhances rather than detracts from your communication.

Avoiding Overuse and Misuse of Slang

While slang can be a powerful tool for self-expression and connection, overusing or misusing it can have the opposite effect. Excessive reliance on slang can make your speech difficult to understand, reduce your credibility, or create an impression of immaturity. To use slang effectively, it's important to strike the right balance and avoid common pitfalls.

One of the most common mistakes is overloading your sentences with slang. While it might seem natural to use multiple trendy expressions in casual conversations, doing so can make your speech feel forced or overwhelming. For example, saying "That party was lit, no cap, it was bussin', and everyone was flexing hard" might confuse someone unfamiliar with the terms, even if they understand the general sentiment.

Instead, try to use slang sparingly and strategically. Choose expressions that add meaning or emphasis to your message rather than filling every sentence with trendy words. This approach not only makes your speech clearer but also ensures that your use of slang feels authentic and purposeful.

Misusing slang is another common issue. Slang often carries specific cultural, generational, or contextual meanings, and using a term incorrectly can make you appear out of touch. For example, misinterpreting "lowkey" (which implies subtlety or moderation) as a synonym for "low effort" could lead to misunderstandings.

To avoid misuse, take the time to observe how others use slang in context before adopting it yourself. Pay attention to the tone, setting, and audience, and don't hesitate to ask for clarification if you're unsure about a term's meaning.

Finally, it's important to recognize when a slang term has become outdated. Language evolves rapidly, and expressions that were once trendy can quickly fall out of favor. Using outdated slang can make you seem disconnected from current culture, so it's essential to stay attuned to linguistic trends and retire terms that no longer resonate.

By being intentional and mindful in your use of slang, you can ensure that it enhances your communication rather than detracting from it.

How to Stay Current with Modern Slang

One of the challenges of using slang is keeping up with its ever-changing nature. New expressions emerge constantly, driven by cultural trends, technological advancements, and generational shifts. Staying current with modern slang requires a combination of observation, engagement, and adaptability.

Social media is one of the most effective tools for staying updated on slang. Platforms like TikTok, Twitter, Instagram, and YouTube are hotbeds of linguistic creativity, with users coining and popularizing new terms daily. By following influencers, creators, and trending hashtags, you can gain insight into the latest slang and see how it's used in real-life contexts. For example, terms like "cap/no cap" and "bussin'" gained widespread popularity through viral videos and memes, making social media an essential resource for staying informed.

Pop culture is another key source of modern slang. Movies, TV shows, music, and gaming communities often introduce phrases that resonate with their audiences and quickly spread to the mainstream. Paying attention to dialogue, lyrics, and cultural references can help you identify emerging trends and incorporate them into your vocabulary.

Engaging with younger generations is also a valuable way to stay current with slang. Teens and young adults are often at the forefront of linguistic innovation, creating and popularizing new expressions that reflect their unique perspectives and experiences. By listening to their conversations, asking questions, and participating in their cultural spaces, you can gain a deeper understanding of contemporary slang and its nuances.

At the same time, it's important to approach slang with an open mind and a willingness to adapt. Language is constantly evolving, and clinging to outdated expressions or resisting new ones can limit your ability to connect with others. Embracing the fluidity of slang allows you to stay relevant and engaged, even as linguistic trends shift over time.

Ultimately, staying current with modern slang is about staying curious and connected. By immersing yourself in the cultural and social contexts that shape language, you can ensure that your use of slang remains fresh, authentic, and effective.

Chapter 9

Fun Slang Quizzes and Exercises

Test Your Slang Knowledge

Engaging with slang can be both educational and entertaining, especially when you challenge yourself to recall and apply what you've learned. Testing your slang knowledge allows you to measure your familiarity with common phrases, recognize the contexts in which they're used, and appreciate the rich diversity of American slang.

To make this fun and interactive, let's start with a quiz. Imagine encountering these questions in a social or casual setting. Can you correctly identify the meanings of these slang terms?

1. What does the term "salty" mean in slang?
a. Tasting like salt
b. Feeling upset or bitter about something
c. Being overly serious
(Answer: b. Feeling upset or bitter about something)

2. If someone says, "That's lit," what do they mean?

a. It's on fire
b. It's exciting, fun, or amazing
c. It's dangerous
(Answer: b. It's exciting, fun, or amazing)

3. What is the meaning of "ghosted"?
a. To disappear or stop responding to someone
b. To scare someone unexpectedly
c. To finish a task quickly
(Answer: a. To disappear or stop responding to someone)

4. In slang, what does "lowkey" imply?
a. Very enthusiastic or excited
b. Subtle, understated, or not overly obvious
c. Having a quiet voice
(Answer: b. Subtle, understated, or not overly obvious)

5. If someone says, "Bet," how are they responding?
a. They agree or confirm
b. They are making a wager
c. They are unsure
(Answer: a. They agree or confirm)

By testing yourself with questions like these, you not only reinforce your understanding of popular slang but also build the confidence to use it effectively in real-life conversations.

Identify the Region: Match the Slang to Its Origin

One of the fascinating aspects of American slang is its regional diversity. Different parts of the United States have developed unique expressions that reflect their local cultures, histories, and identities. Recognizing the origins of slang can deepen your appreciation for the richness of the language.

Let's play a matching game. Below are popular slang terms, followed by regions they're commonly associated with. Can you match each slang word to its origin?

Slang Terms:

Y'all

Hella

Jawn

Ope

Wicked

Regions:

1. West Coast

2. Northeast

3. Midwest

4. Southern United States

Answers:

Y'all → Southern United States: A contraction of "you all," this term is widely used in the South as an inclusive way to address a group of people.

Hella → West Coast: Originating from Northern California, "hella" means "a lot" or "very."

Jawn → Northeast: Specifically popular in Philadelphia, "jawn" is a versatile term used to describe almost anything, from a person to an object.

Ope → Midwest: A common Midwestern interjection used when bumping into someone or making a small mistake, as in, "Ope, didn't see you there!"

Wicked → Northeast: Especially common in New England, "wicked" is used to intensify adjectives, as in "wicked awesome."

By engaging in activities like this, you gain insight into the cultural and geographical influences on American slang. It's a fun way to explore how language varies across regions while testing your knowledge of local expressions.

Fill-in-the-Blank Exercises

Another enjoyable way to practice slang is through fill-in-the-blank exercises. These challenges encourage you to think critically about the context and meaning of slang terms, helping you solidify your understanding.

Complete the sentences below using the correct slang word from the options provided:

1. When Sarah found out she got the job, she was so _____________.
(Options: salty, lit, stoked)
(Answer: stoked)

2. I tried to message him, but he totally _____________ me.
(Options: ghosted, flexed, chilled)
(Answer: ghosted)

3. The party last night was ___________. Everyone had a great time!
(Options: sus, bussin', lit)
(Answer: lit)

4. I'm ___________ heading to the concert, but I still need to check my schedule.
(Options: lowkey, bet, extra)
(Answer: lowkey)

5. The price for this jacket is a ___________. I can't believe it's so cheap!
(Options: steal, chill, rip-off)
(Answer: steal)

Fill-in-the-blank exercises like these are an interactive way to reinforce your knowledge of slang while having fun with the creative possibilities of language.

Slang in Conversations: Practice Scenarios

Applying slang in realistic conversations is one of the best ways to develop fluency and confidence. Practice scenarios allow you to experiment with slang in different contexts, helping you understand when and how to use these expressions naturally.

Imagine the following situations. How would you respond using appropriate slang?

Scenario 1: At a Party
Your friend asks how you're enjoying the event. You want to express that you're having an amazing time.

Response: "This party is lit! I'm so glad I came."

Scenario 2: Online Messaging
A friend texts you to share exciting news about a promotion. How do you congratulate them?

Response: "That's awesome! You totally crushed it. Congrats!"

Scenario 3: Shopping
You're at a store and find an item at an unbelievably low price. How do you express your excitement to a friend?

Response: "This jacket is such a steal—I can't believe it's only $20!"

Scenario 4: Travel Plans
Your friends are planning a road trip and ask if you're interested in joining. You're enthusiastic about the idea.

Response: "I'm so down for this road trip—it's going to be epic!"

Scenario 5: Dealing with Disappointment
You're upset because a restaurant you wanted to try is closed. How do you share your feelings?

Response: "I'm so salty about this—they had such good reviews."

Practicing scenarios like these helps you become more comfortable using slang in everyday conversations. Over time, you'll develop a natural sense of when and where certain expressions fit best.

By combining quizzes, matching games, fill-in-the-blank exercises, and conversation scenarios, you can transform learning slang into an enjoyable and interactive experience. These activities not only reinforce your knowledge but also build your confidence in using slang effectively, making your communication more dynamic and relatable.

Chapter 10

The Future of American Slang

How Slang Will Continue to Evolve

Language is a living entity, constantly adapting to the changing needs and experiences of its users. Slang, in particular, reflects this fluidity more than any other aspect of language. It captures the pulse of society—its culture, technology, and collective psyche—shaping and being shaped by the way people interact. As we look to the future of American slang, one thing is certain: it will continue to evolve, adapting to the new realities and influences of the digital age, global connectivity, and social transformation.

The evolution of slang is driven by several key factors. Social changes, for instance, often bring about shifts in language. As new cultural movements emerge and marginalized voices gain visibility, these groups contribute unique linguistic expressions that often become mainstream. Consider how the LGBTQ+ community introduced terms like "shade" and "slay" into popular vernacular, or how African American Vernacular English (AAVE) has been a powerful influence on modern slang through hip-hop culture. As social justice movements and diversity continue to shape American society, we can expect a rich influx of expressions that reflect these evolving identities.

Technology is another critical driver of linguistic change. As people increasingly communicate through digital platforms, the way they use language adapts to these new mediums. Shortened phrases, emojis, and abbreviations have already transformed the way we express emotions, humor, and even sarcasm online. In the future, as technologies like augmented reality (AR) and virtual reality (VR) become more integrated into daily life, new slang may emerge to describe experiences unique to these platforms.

The rise of artificial intelligence could also influence slang. As people interact more frequently with AI-driven tools, new expressions might develop to describe these interactions or critique the role of AI in society. For instance, terms for AI malfunctions, ethical dilemmas, or even specific AI-generated content could enter everyday speech.

Another hallmark of slang's evolution is its cyclical nature. Just as fashion trends often resurface with a modern twist, slang from past decades could reappear in unexpected ways. However, these recycled expressions often carry new meanings or nuances shaped by the current cultural context. Words like "rad" and "groovy" may return to popularity among younger generations, but they might be used ironically or to evoke nostalgia.

Ultimately, slang will continue to evolve as a reflection of the human experience, adapting to the social, cultural, and technological landscapes of the future.

Predictions for the Next Generation of Expressions

Predicting the future of slang is both an art and a science. While we can't know exactly what expressions will emerge, we can identify trends and cultural shifts that are likely to influence the next generation of slang.

One major influence will be the continued integration of technology into everyday life. As the lines between the physical and digital worlds blur, new slang terms will likely arise to describe these hybrid experiences. For instance, as AR and VR become commonplace, we may see expressions for things like "digital hangouts," where friends meet in virtual spaces, or "avatar envy," a term for wanting a better online persona.

The rise of environmental awareness and sustainability efforts could also inspire new slang. Younger generations, particularly Gen Z and Gen Alpha, are deeply engaged with climate issues, and their advocacy may lead to the creation of terms that reflect their priorities. Phrases like "eco-flex" (showing off environmentally friendly choices) or "green ghosting" (ignoring companies with unsustainable practices) could emerge as part of this movement.

Cultural diversity will remain a significant driver of new slang. As globalization continues to bring people from different backgrounds together, American slang will likely incorporate more words and phrases from other languages. We're already seeing examples of this with terms like "hygge" (a Danish word for coziness) and "kawaii" (a Japanese word for cuteness). In the future, this trend may expand as young people adopt and adapt words from cultures they encounter through travel, media, or online communities.

Generational differences will also play a major role in shaping new slang. Younger generations often develop their own linguistic codes to distinguish themselves from their elders. These codes are heavily influenced by the cultural touchstones of their time, from viral memes to popular music. As Gen Alpha comes of age, they will create expressions that reflect their unique worldview, influenced by their upbringing in an era of constant connectivity and rapid technological change.

Another trend to watch is the growing intersection between slang and visual communication. Emojis, GIFs, and memes already play a significant role in modern communication, often serving as shorthand for complex emotions or ideas. In the future, slang may increasingly incorporate visual elements, with specific combinations of symbols or images serving as new forms of expression. For instance, a certain emoji sequence could come to represent an inside joke or a shared cultural reference.

While the specific words and phrases of tomorrow are impossible to predict, one thing is clear: they will reflect the creativity, ingenuity, and diversity of the people who use them.

Global Influence on American Slang

Slang has always been a dynamic, porous aspect of language, absorbing influences from a variety of sources. In the modern era, globalization has accelerated this process, allowing slang to cross borders and cultures more easily than ever before. American slang, in particular, is increasingly shaped by global influences, creating a rich and evolving linguistic tapestry.

The internet has played a pivotal role in this global exchange of language. Social media platforms, online gaming, and streaming services have connected people from different countries, exposing them to each other's slang. As a result, terms from other languages and cultures often find their way into American English. For example, words like "hombre" (Spanish for man) and "schnitzel" (German for a type of food) have long been part of American vernacular, but the digital age has introduced newer terms like "kilig" (a Filipino word for a feeling of romantic excitement) and "gezellig" (a Dutch word for a cozy and enjoyable atmosphere).

Music and entertainment are also major drivers of global influence on American slang. The popularity of genres like K-pop, reggaeton, and Afrobeat has introduced fans to the linguistic nuances of these cultures, while international films and TV shows expose audiences to phrases they might not have encountered otherwise. As these cultural exports continue to gain traction in the U.S., they will likely contribute new words and expressions to the American slang lexicon.

Immigration is another key factor in the globalization of American slang. The U.S. has long been a melting pot of cultures, and this diversity is reflected in its language. Immigrant communities bring their own linguistic traditions, which often blend with existing American slang to create something entirely new. For example, Spanglish—a mix of Spanish and English—has given rise to expressions like "no manches" (a phrase expressing disbelief) and "chela" (a casual term for beer). As immigration patterns continue to evolve, so too will the contributions of these communities to American slang.

Global events and movements also play a role in shaping slang. The COVID-19 pandemic, for example, introduced a host of new terms and phrases into everyday language, many of which originated outside the U.S. Words like "quarantine" and "lockdown" became universally understood, while terms like "quaranteam" (a group of people quarantining together) reflected the creativity and adaptability of slang during challenging times.

Looking to the future, the global influence on American slang is likely to deepen as technology continues to shrink the distance between cultures. This cross-pollination of language will enrich American slang, making it more diverse, inclusive, and representative of a connected world.

American slang, shaped by its past and present influences, is on a trajectory of endless evolution. As society changes, so too will the expressions we use to describe it. By examining how slang reflects our culture, predicts our future, and connects us to the world, we gain a deeper appreciation for the vibrancy and creativity of language. The future of American slang is as unpredictable as it is exciting, promising new ways to express ourselves in an ever-changing world.

Glossary of American Slang Terms

Alphabetical List of Slang Terms with Meanings and Examples

Slang is a vibrant and ever-evolving component of the English language, capturing the essence of cultural moments and everyday experiences. Below is a comprehensive alphabetical glossary of American slang terms, complete with meanings and examples of usage. This section is designed to not only educate but also entertain, offering readers a glimpse into the rich and colorful world of informal language.

A

Ace – To perform exceptionally well, often on a test or task.
Example: "I aced that math exam. It was way easier than I expected."

All-nighter – Staying up all night to study, work, or complete a task.
Example: "We pulled an all-nighter to finish the project, but it was worth it."

Awks – Short for "awkward," often used in casual or humorous situations.
Example: "It was so awks when I accidentally waved back at a stranger."

B

Bet – A term of agreement or confirmation, similar to "okay" or "sure."
Example: "You want to grab pizza tonight? Bet!"

Busted – Used to describe something broken or someone caught doing something wrong.
Example: "His phone is busted; he needs a new one."

Bougie – Derived from "bourgeois," it refers to someone or something fancy, pretentious, or high-class.
Example: "She's so bougie with her designer handbags and fancy coffee orders."

C

Cap/No Cap – "Cap" means a lie, and "no cap" means being truthful.
Example: "He said he could run a mile in five minutes—definitely cap."

Chill – To relax or be easygoing.
Example: "Let's just chill at home tonight and watch a movie."

Clapback – A quick, witty, or snarky retort in response to criticism.

Example: "Her clapback was so good, he didn't know what to say."

D
Dead – Used to express extreme amusement, often meaning "I'm dying of laughter."
Example: "That meme was so funny, I'm dead!"

Dope – Cool, excellent, or amazing.
Example: "That new album is dope—you should listen to it!"

Drop the ball – To fail or make a mistake, especially when it was avoidable.
Example: "I totally dropped the ball on organizing the meeting."

E
Extra – Over the top, dramatic, or excessive.
Example: "She's being so extra about her birthday party decorations."

Epic – Incredible or amazing, often describing something grand or adventurous.
Example: "Our road trip across the country was epic!"

F
Flex – To show off or boast about something.
Example: "He's always flexing his new sneakers on Instagram."

Fire – Amazing, excellent, or extremely good.
Example: "That new song is fire; I can't stop playing it!"

G
Ghosted – To suddenly cut off communication with someone, usually in a dating context.
Example: "I thought we were getting along, but then he ghosted me."

Gnarly – Awesome or cool, but can also mean intense or severe.
Example: "That wave was gnarly! I've never seen anything like it."

Go-to – A favorite or reliable option.
Example: "Pizza is my go-to meal when I don't feel like cooking."

H
Hella – Very or a lot; commonly used on the West Coast.
Example: "That party was hella fun; we stayed until 2 a.m."

Hit up – To contact someone, usually by phone or text.
Example: "Hit me up later if you want to hang out."

Hype – Excitement or anticipation, often about an event or product.
Example: "The hype around this movie is unreal—it better be good!"

I

I'm down – An expression of agreement or willingness.
Example: "You want to go hiking this weekend? I'm down!"

In the bag – Something that is certain or guaranteed.
Example: "With that final goal, the game is in the bag."

J

Janky – Low-quality, unreliable, or broken.
Example: "This old laptop is so janky; it crashes every five minutes."

Jawn – A versatile term used in Philadelphia to refer to anything or anyone.
Example: "Pass me that jawn on the table."

Juiced – Excited or enthusiastic.
Example: "I'm so juiced for the concert tonight!"

K

Karen – A term for an entitled or overly demanding person, often used to describe someone causing a scene.
Example: "That Karen in the store demanded to speak to the manager."

Keep it 100 – To be completely honest or authentic.
Example: "I'm going to keep it 100 with you—that outfit doesn't match."

Kick it – To hang out or relax with someone.
Example: "We're just going to kick it at my place tonight."

L
Lit – Exciting, fun, or amazing.
Example: "The concert last night was lit; the crowd went wild!"

Lowkey – Subtle or understated; not wanting to draw attention.
Example: "I'm lowkey excited about the new movie, but I don't want to overhype it."

M
Mad – Used as an intensifier to mean "very" or "a lot."
Example: "That pizza was mad good—I need to order it again."

Mood – Something relatable or that describes how you feel.
Example: "That cat lying in bed all day is such a mood."

N
Noob – A beginner or someone inexperienced, often in gaming contexts.
Example: "He's such a noob at this game—he keeps losing!"

On point – Perfect, flawless, or well-executed.

Example: "Her outfit is on point today—she looks amazing!"

Ope – A Midwestern interjection used when bumping into someone or making a mistake.
Example: "Ope, didn't see you there!"

P
Pop – The Midwestern term for soda or soft drink.
Example: "Do you want a pop with your meal?"

Plug – A person who supplies something, often tickets or exclusive items.
Example: "He's the plug for all the best concert seats."

Q
Quirky – Unconventional, unique, or eccentric in an endearing way.
Example: "Her quirky sense of humor always makes me laugh."

R
Rad – Short for radical, meaning cool or awesome.
Example: "That skateboard trick was totally rad!"

Ripped off – Overcharged or scammed.
Example: "I feel like I got ripped off paying $50 for that meal."

S
Salty – Upset, bitter, or annoyed about something.

Example: "He's still salty about losing the game last night."

Savage – Bold, daring, or brutally honest.
Example: "Her comeback to that insult was savage!"

T
Throw shade – To subtly insult or criticize someone.
Example: "She's always throwing shade at her coworkers during meetings."

Turnt – Very excited, energetic, or intoxicated.
Example: "The party got turnt after the DJ started playing our favorite songs."

U
Up in the air – Something uncertain or undecided.
Example: "The plans for the weekend are still up in the air."

V
Vibes – The emotional atmosphere or feeling of a place or situation.
Example: "This café has such good vibes—it's so relaxing."

W
Wicked – Extremely or very, commonly used in New England.
Example: "That rollercoaster was wicked fast!"

Woke – Aware of social and political issues, especially injustices.
Example: "She's so woke when it comes to environmental activism."

Y

Y'all – A contraction of "you all," commonly used in the Southern United States.
Example: "Are y'all coming to the barbecue this weekend?"

Z

Zonked – Extremely tired or exhausted.
Example: "After working all day, I'm completely zonked."

This glossary provides just a snapshot of the creative and colorful world of American slang. By exploring these terms, you can deepen your understanding of informal language and its role in shaping everyday communication. Slang, after all, is more than just words—it's a reflection of culture, identity, and shared experience.

Conclusion

Final Thoughts on the Power of Slang

Slang is far more than a collection of informal words and phrases; it is a powerful tool that transcends mere communication. It reflects the dynamic, ever-changing fabric of society and embodies the creativity, resilience, and humor of human expression. From its origins in small, localized communities to its global presence in the digital age, slang tells the story of who we are as individuals and as a collective. It reveals the values, struggles, and triumphs of a generation and serves as a mirror to cultural shifts.

Slang has the unique ability to bring people together. It fosters a sense of belonging, creating an unspoken bond among those who understand its nuances. When someone uses slang that resonates with their social group, it sends a subtle but powerful message: "I get you." This shared understanding strengthens relationships, whether between friends, colleagues, or even strangers who recognize a common linguistic thread. It is no wonder that slang continues to flourish, despite its informal and often fleeting nature.

Moreover, slang has an undeniable role in breaking down barriers. Across regions, socioeconomic backgrounds, and even languages, slang serves as a bridge that connects people. It is a linguistic melting pot where influences from music, movies, social media, and diverse cultures come together to create something new and inclusive. In many ways, slang is a testament to the human desire to innovate and adapt, using language as a tool to reflect our shared humanity.

At its core, slang is an art form. The creativity involved in coining a new term, giving it life, and watching it spread is a fascinating process. It often starts with a single person or a small group and quickly gains momentum, capturing the imagination of an entire community or even the world. Every time we use slang, we participate in this creative process, contributing to the ever-evolving tapestry of language. It is this constant evolution that makes slang so exciting—it is never static, always changing to reflect the times.

As we've explored throughout this book, slang is deeply rooted in culture, history, and human connection. From the timeless expressions of the past to the digital slang of today, it is clear that slang will continue to play a vital role in communication. It is a living, breathing part of language, always adapting to the needs and influences of each generation. Recognizing its power allows us to appreciate its significance and understand its impact on how we interact with the world around us.

Encouragement to Keep Learning and Using Slang

As we close this exploration of American slang, the journey doesn't end here—it is just the beginning. Language is a lifelong adventure, and slang is one of its most exciting and dynamic components. There is always something new to learn, whether it's a phrase from a bygone era, a regional expression you've never heard before, or the latest term sweeping social media. Embracing slang not only enriches your vocabulary but also deepens your cultural awareness and strengthens your connections with others.

The beauty of slang lies in its accessibility. Unlike formal language, which often requires years of study and practice, slang invites everyone to participate. It is a language of the people, constantly shaped by the voices of everyday life. Whether you're a linguistics enthusiast, a casual observer, or someone eager to connect with others on a deeper level, there is a place for you in the world of slang.

Using slang is also an act of engagement with the world around you. By incorporating it into your speech, you demonstrate your awareness of cultural trends and your willingness to adapt. It shows that you are not afraid to experiment with language, to try something new, and to connect with others in a way that feels genuine and relevant. It is a reminder that language is not just about rules and structure; it is about expression, creativity, and connection.

As you continue to learn and use slang, remember that it is not about being perfect or always staying on top of the latest trends. Slang is meant to be fun, playful, and reflective of your personality. Use it as a tool to express yourself, to bring humor and color into your conversations, and to bond with those around you. And don't be afraid to make mistakes—after all, language is a journey, not a destination.

Staying current with slang doesn't have to feel like a chore. It can be as simple as listening to how others speak, exploring social media trends, or immersing yourself in music, movies, and other forms of pop culture. Pay attention to the words and phrases that resonate with you and incorporate them into your everyday life. The more you use slang, the more natural it will feel, and the more you will appreciate its versatility and charm.

Ultimately, the power of slang lies in its ability to make language accessible, engaging, and endlessly fascinating. It encourages us to step outside of the confines of traditional speech and explore new ways of communicating. It reminds us that language is not just about conveying information; it is about sharing experiences, building relationships, and expressing who we are.

As you close this book, take with you not only a deeper understanding of American slang but also an appreciation for its role in shaping the way we communicate. Let this handbook be a starting point—a gateway to a world of linguistic creativity and cultural exploration. Whether you are mastering classic expressions, diving into regional dialects, or experimenting with the latest Gen Z terms, know that you are part of a larger conversation, one that transcends borders, generations, and cultures.

Slang is a celebration of language in its most playful and human form. It is a reminder that words have power—not just to inform, but to inspire, connect, and transform. So go forth with confidence, curiosity, and a sense of adventure. Keep learning, keep using, and, most importantly, keep enjoying the vibrant, ever-changing world of slang.